HUMBLE *Beginnings*

The National Theatre at Work

Robert Butler

The Author

Robert Butler is a freelance journalist. From 1995-2000 he was drama critic of the *Independent on Sunday*

To Sarah

Thanks to Tim de Lisle and Marie-Christine Willis for reading a draft

Humble Beginnings is published by
NT Publications
Royal National Theatre
South Bank, London SE1 9PX
www.nationaltheatre.org.uk
in association with The Caird Company
publishing@cairdcompany.com

Editor Lyn Haill
Designer Stephen Cummiskey
Photographs by Catherine Ashmore
Rehearsal drawings by Andrew Tyzack
Typeset in Agenda

Humble Beginnings is the second in the series 'The National Theatre at Work'. The first was Jonathan Croall's *Hamlet Observed*; and the next is his *Inside the Molly House*. Di Trevis' *Remembrance of Things Proust* also explores the process of putting on a play at the National

Printed by Battley Brothers, Clapham, London SW4 OJN

ISBN No. 0 9519943 6 0

The Cast

Humble Boy

by **Charlotte Jones**

Felix Humble	**Simon Russell Beale**
Mercy Lott	**Marcia Warren**
Flora Humble	**Diana Rigg**
Jim the gardener	**William Gaunt**
George Pye	**Denis Quilley**
Rosie Pye	**Cathryn Bradshaw**

Music played by **Charlotte Bradburn** (Music Director/saxophone), **Adam Caird** (piano), **Zoë Martlew** (cello)

Director	**John Caird**
Designer	**Tim Hatley**
Associate Costume Designer	**Lucy Roberts**
Lighting Designer	**Paul Pyant**
Music	**Joe Cutler**
Sound Designer	**Christopher Shutt**
Company Voice Work	**Patsy Rodenburg**

Production Manager
Diane Willmott

Deputy Stage Manager
Fiona Bardsley

Assistant to the Designer
Libby Watson

Production Intern
Richard Gorr

Stage Manager
Trish Montemuro

Assistant Stage Manager
Valerie Fox, Andrew Speed

Assistant to the Lighting Designer
Elaine Grimes

Production Photographer
Catherine Ashmore

Opening the Cottesloe Theatre 9 August 2001

Humble Boy *was presented at the National in association with Matthew Byam Shaw and Anna Mackmin*

The production was supported by the Peter Wolff Theatre Trust

Humble Beginnings

- ***Warning: this account of the rehearsals of* Humble Boy *gives away most of the plot***

- The next chapter of this book – describing the play's opening and reception – is published on the National Theatre's website at www.nationaltheatre.org.uk/publications

- *What occurs between the characters in* Humble Boy *is described in the present tense. What occurred between the company during rehearsals is described in the past tense*

Humble *Beginnings*

THE OPENING OF A NEW PLAY AT THE NATIONAL IS QUITE UNLIKE ANY OTHER EVENING IN THE THEATRE. In one way, it's real enough: there is a new play; there are actors; there is an audience. In another way, it is what has been termed a *pseudo-event*. What surrounds the new play is a drama that is as choreographed as the play itself.

If you had walked past the stage door of the Royal National Theatre on a mild summer's evening – 13 June 2001, to be precise – you might have noticed a white table just inside the stage door entrance. It was covered with flowers, champagne and envelopes that were placed next to stickers with the names Patrick, Ron, Ashley, Cherry, Trevor, Paul, Nadim, Mossie, Russell, Benedict and Elian. About 70 yards further on, the First Night crowd was gathering on the steps of the National's smallest theatre, the Cottesloe. If you had stepped inside the foyer you might have discovered that most of the members of the audience knew one another. Over by the snazzy new box office, that looks like a check-in desk at British Airways, the press officers were handing out complimentary tickets. Everyone seemed to get one. Nearby, a crisply-dressed literary agent was warmly greeting a laid-back West End producer. *She* represents the playwright. *He* produced the playwright's last work on Broadway. In the centre of the foyer four critics from national newspapers gossiped over a drink – the combined circulation of their papers is six million. And by the concrete staircase, a woman who lives with one of the actors in tonight's play was fixing to have lunch with one of the younger female critics (circulation: 250,000), and over there –

– the three minute bell. This very familiar audience of 300 shuffled through two sets of double doors into the auditorium. In the aisle seats, critics dug out notebooks and pens. The lights came up on stage, an actor walked on and said *Hey, mate. Mate? You got a spare?* and it had started. Another new play at the National... a routine occurrence in so many lives... but not for the playwright.

In two hours' time, when it was still light and warm outside, some critics would walk to their newspaper offices and others would be escorted to rooms within the National and provided with a drink – it had already been ordered – and a desk. An hour after the show, the first verdicts on this latest play had been filed and by breakfast the next day people were able to say, *I hear there's a new compassion, I hear he's gone soft*. The National receives about a thousand new plays a year and only a tiny fraction are ever staged, from Peter Shaffer's *The Royal Hunt of The Sun* in 1964 to Patrick Marber's *Howard Katz*, the world premiere that night.

Twelve days later, on 25 June, another new play went into rehearsal at the National – this one was called *Humble Boy* – and six weeks after that, on 9 August, the white table was back at the stage door entrance, covered with flowers, champagne and envelopes, this time placed next to stickers with the names Charlotte, Diana, Simon, Denis, Marcia, William, Cathryn and John. The First Night crowd gathered on the steps of the Cottesloe, chatted in the foyer, shuffled through two sets of double doors, and the critics dug out their notebooks and pens. The lights went up on stage, an actor walked on and said – *The b– b– b– bees have gone* – and it had started again... another new play at the National... a routine occurrence... but not for the playwright.

Her name is Charlotte Jones. Her last play *Martha, Josie and the Chinese Elvis* was performed at the Bolton Octagon in Greater Manchester and the one before that, *In Flame*, opened at the London fringe theatre, the Bush and – months later – it transferred to the West End. Her plays are broadcast on Radio 4... but *Humble Boy... Humble Boy* is her first play at the National and what happens at the National gets noticed around the world. If it goes well, it will join the A-list and may be performed in New York or Los Angeles or Vancouver or Sydney or Birmingham or Leeds or Manchester or Dublin or – once it has been translated – Munich or Oslo or Haifa or Paris or Stockholm. And that means... what exactly? Ask the National Theatre's literary manager, Jack Bradley, and his answer is simple. *It will transform her life.*

THERE ARE two ways to get a new play on at the National. One is the direct route. Your name is Harold Pinter. Your agent sends a copy of your latest play to the National. The artistic director and the literary manager read the script that night and the next morning they ring and say that your play is absolutely fantastic and they want to put it on as soon as they can schedule it.

The other way is the indirect route. Charlotte Jones and her husband, Paul Bazely, had gone to see the film *American Beauty* and, afterwards, they were walking back to the tube station at Earls Court when Bazely got a call from his agent. He said to his wife, "I've just been offered Guildenstern at the National" and she said, "What do you think?" and he said "Guess who's playing Hamlet?" His wife had been to the National's productions of *Summerfolk* and *Battle Royal* just to see this actor – one of the most intelligent and entertaining of his generation – so Bazely knew it would interest her. This actor had been in her mind when she was writing her new play. Bazely told his wife who was playing Hamlet and she thought, *I can't believe this. It has to be a sign.*

Charlotte Jones didn't want to put any pressure on her husband but she couldn't help thinking of a number of good reasons why he should play Guildenstern... let's see... it was the National, the director was John Caird, the lead actor was Simon Russell Beale, and really, Guildenstern is not an insignificant role. No emotional blackmail, nothing to tip the scales, no murmurings along the lines of: *my play! my play! what about my play?* –

– because, right then, her play was stuck. After the success of *In Flame*, the director and the producer of that production, Anna Mackmin and Matthew Byam Shaw, had taken Charlotte Jones out to a swanky lunch and commissioned her to write another play. When Charlotte Jones had finished *Humble Boy*, the three of them agreed that the Cottesloe would be the perfect venue and they sent a copy to the literary manager at the National, and he had read it and said he liked it, and he showed it to the artistic director, Trevor Nunn, and he read it and said he liked it, and he wrote to Charlotte Jones and said that he hoped the National would be able to produce it. The only snag was that the National would not be able to produce it within the immediate time-frame. We love your play... we're just not putting it on...

Luckily, Bazely wanted to be in *Hamlet*. During rehearsals he went up to Russell Beale and said that his wife had written a play and she was very keen for Russell Beale to take a look at it. He handed over a copy of *Humble Boy*. Inside there was a note, *whether you like it or not, I had you in my head when I was writing it. You are my dream Felix. Thanks for the inspiration.* Russell Beale knew that he had seen the script before – a producer had sent it to him or an agent had or both – and he had thought that he had liked it or had liked what he had read of it, but since he doesn't trust his own judgment over new scripts, really he doesn't, he thinks he is a terrible reader – a *crap* one, to be frank – he had done nothing about it. This time he took the play home and did nothing about it again.

A few weeks later John Caird, the director of the National's productions of *Candide* and *Hamlet*, held a party in his house in Highgate for the casts of *Candide* and *Hamlet* and the author of *Humble Boy* was invited because she was the wife of the actor playing Guildenstern. It was her first meeting with her future director and her first meeting with her dream Felix. Russell Beale thanked her for her note... so he had obviously read that... it just wasn't very clear if he had read the play, and if he had, whether he had liked it.

Before *Hamlet* opened at the National it went on tour. When the company was in Malvern, Bazely again asked Russell Beale about the script and now that Russell Beale had done a few performances and had a little more time he said that hewould like to look at it again. Only he hadn't brought his copy. *No problem,* said Bazely, *have mine.* Over the next few months, as he performed the role of Guildenstern, who listens out for clues to Hamlet's thoughts and reports them back to the King and Queen, Bazely also listened out for clues to Russell Beale's thoughts about *Humble Boy* and reported them back to his wife. In their flat in Putney, West London, each twist in the play's fortunes within the National was scrutinised. The impression was that if Simon wanted to do it, the National would do it – Russell Beale has a big following among the South Bank audience – but what did Simon want?

The character of Felix is a 35-year old astrophysicist who is contemplating suicide. One phrase in the play that appealed to Russell Beale was the description of his character as *overweight but not unattractive*. It was an improvement on film roles that he goes up for where he finds the character he has been asked to read is described as *fat*, *camp* or *idiotic*. He also liked the way the play was a happy *Hamlet*: Felix survives.

Russell Beale had made his reputation playing distinctive sharp-edged characters – Iago, Richard III, Oswald in *Ghosts.* When he had been rehearsing *The Duchess of Malfi*, another member of the cast, Juliet Stevenson, gave him some simple advice, *Stop worrying about the effect you're having*. An actor has to have a third eye, has to be aware of what he or she is doing, but an actor can also have the confidence that what his or her character is thinking or feeling is simply interesting in itself. This had been a tip that Russell Beale was able to use as he rehearsed and performed *Hamlet*. He felt it was a step forward. When he read *Humble Boy* he kept that lesson in mind. Here was a contemporary character within whom a great deal was happening. He thought playing Felix might be a way of following up on what he had learnt. He sent the play *upstairs...* to the fourth floor of the National where the decisions are taken. He didn't champion the script, he didn't argue for it, he didn't even say he liked it. He said he *thought* he liked it.

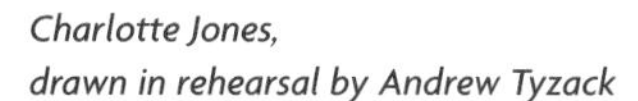

Charlotte Jones,
drawn in rehearsal by Andrew Tyzack

BACK IN the West End, the producer who had commissioned the play, Matthew Byam Shaw, had a script and no theatre... so he... so he... so he held a rehearsed reading... not one of those warm, supportive script-development sessions, but a hard sell to the men in suits and the women in black. He organised this reading around a number of brisk principles:

- Make it select. Invite people who are in competition with one another.
- Put the audience on the same level as the actors and keep the lights up. (*We can see you!)*
- Don't allow people to sit in cliques. If a theatre owner arrives with a theatre manager – and they've probably just had lunch in The Ivy – separate them. They won't like it. They'll think it's rude. But do it all the same.
- Make sure the script isn't longer than one hour 45 minutes. Make sure it has laughs.
- Within two minutes of the reading finishing, have a glass of Sauvignon blanc in everyone's hand.

The venue was a room in the Old Vic and the turn-out was good... West End, film, television and radio producers, agents and representatives from the Royal Court, the Donmar Warehouse and the West Yorkshire Playhouse... they had been attracted by the critical praise for *In Flame* and the names doing the reading: Simon Russell Beale, Denis Quilley, Marcia Warren, Patricia Hodge, Sarah Woodward and Clive Merrison. The cast were chauffeured to and from their homes and given top-of-the-range sandwiches and Sauvignon blanc for lunch. No-one from the National was there. It was the height of the rail crisis, when every other train was running slow, and Jack Bradley was stuck on one back from Sheffield.

Humble Boy opens on the day of James Humble's funeral. A neighbour is talking to the son, Felix Humble. For the first few minutes of the reading Byam Shaw was worrying as three cracking lines – as they say – *went for nothing*... then Mrs Humble entered the garden. Her son had walked out on his own father's funeral. She was recovering from plastic surgery on her nose. The conflict between mother and son was instant. The audience twigged that this was a play about breaking social taboos. As he was reading it, Russell Beale was surprised... people were laughing, the play was funny, the lunch scene was very funny –

– from the start, Charlotte Jones had felt sick... it was like an auction where no-one was bidding... right in front of her she could see a distinguished theatre agent fast asleep... a producer came up to her afterwards and said that it needed *a lot* of rewrites... no-one seemed to express any real interest in putting on her play... it was... oh god... uuuuuurrrrrrrrrrrggggghhhhhhHHHHHH!!!!!

John Caird

BUT THE West Yorkshire Playhouse was very interested in the play, so Matthew Byam Shaw went back over the bridge to the National and asked for a yes or a no. The answer was a long time coming. Charlotte Jones insisted that Byam Shaw say no to the West Yorkshire Playhouse. If there was a chance of a London production, she was determined to take it. Her view was that a writer who wants a *career as a playwright* has to have a London production. For five weeks they sat around with their fingers crossed. The situation was changing at the National as a couple of productions had done badly at the box office and spaces for new productions were now becoming available. The National said it would want to choose its own director and a copy of *Humble Boy* was sent to John Caird, the director of *Hamlet* and *Candide* and host of the party in Highgate. He read the play and thought it was funny and ironic and allusive and charming. It was poetic, but in a colloquial way. It was very English too. *Humble Boy* now had a powerful friend on the fourth floor.

When Caird had lunch with Charlotte Jones, he said that if he directed it he would want her to be there for every day of rehearsals. He thought one of the most depressing developments over the last 50 years had been the rise of the director as *auteur.* He deplored the way writers were kept out of rehearsals – often invited in for the first read-through and then told to come back in three weeks. Keeping the writer out of rehearsals was usually a mark of insecurity and immaturity on the part of directors. Personally he loved it when an actor came up to him in rehearsals and said, *You said such and such to me but I've just spoken to the author and he/she says that my character would do such and such...* he just loved it when they did that... because often when you sat down and talked about the character and what the character did you found that *both things were true*. If Charlotte wanted to talk to any of the actors about their roles during rehearsals or go round to their dressing-rooms during the run and talk about the performances and say something that was different from anything he had said... that was absolutely fine...

THE FIRST day of rehearsals was the first day of Wimbledon. At the National the cast would be able to catch a bit of the tennis on the televisions at the stage door and in the Green Room bar. It was a hot Monday morning and Rehearsal Room 3 at the National is a large hexagonal room with no windows, lit by fluorescent lights that lie in rows between the air ducts. This is a room that has missed its true calling as a level in a multi-storey car park. To alleviate the dreary atmosphere the stage managers had brought in four 'floods' that bounced light off the ceiling. Some of the most talented actors in the country would spend the best five weeks of the summer in Rehearsal Room 3.

Humble Boy is a play for six characters and there were 40 people in the room. John Caird welcomed everyone and said that usually Trevor Nunn made a speech at the beginning of rehearsals, explaining that the National is one big family, but Nunn had a board meeting this morning, so Caird had just said it for him. He suggested that everyone in the room introduce themselves, which they did, from press officer to production manager to musician to actor to playwright to composer to stage manager to marketing manager to costume designer to casting director to head of publications to nurse to sound engineer: the responsibilities ran from the buzz in the media to the buzz of the bumblebees. A black cloth was lifted off a black box to reveal the model of the set. It was a garden with tall grass – made from the bristles of a brush – surrounding a tiled patio. The set was completely green. At the back of the stage these bristles ran up several levels in row after row to a beehive. *Non-naturalism* was the term. William Gaunt, playing the gardener, studied the bristles with interest: "He's obviously not a very successful gardener."

A few miles away, in an industrial estate off the Old Kent Road, three women were standing behind trestle tables next to a stack of boxes that contained the tall grass. The women took each blade of grass and glued it to a narrow green strip. The boxes had been imported from Germany, but where the grass had originally come from, no-one knew... somewhere temperate, they imagined... Vietnam or Indonesia. The grass had been dried and dyed and once the three women had attached the grass to the strips of tape – the job would take them four weeks – the grass would hang from the workshop wall, where it would be doused with fire-resistant spray. It would then be inserted in narrow channels that had been incised in polystyrene flooring. This polystyrene would run round the edge of the set. The effect would be like the soft willowy grass that grows near the edge of lakes. Those members of the audience with front row seats would watch the play through the tips of the blades of grass. The design by Tim Hatley would cost £30,000, which was within budget.

After coffee, the cast of *Humble Boy* sat round the four tables that had been pushed together in the centre. The cast brought a variety of traditions to these four tables, from tragedy to farce to musicals to sitcoms. There were long-standing professional relationships and brand new ones. John Caird likes ensembles and continuities: the trunks, and the idea of travelling, that he used in his production of *Candide* reappeared in his production of *Hamlet*. (There was an idea that the two would tour together.) There were actors who reappeared too. Three members of the *Hamlet* company were appearing in *Humble Boy*. The four members of the stage management team, led by Trish Montemuro, had stage managed *Hamlet*. Three of the actors from the read-through were appearing in *Humble Boy*. Of the other three actors, William Gaunt had joined the National to play the father in *Look Back in Anger* and stayed for *The Mysteries, Albert Speer, The Cherry Orchard*... and now *Humble Boy*. Marcia Warren had been in the two productions of Charlotte Jones' *In Flame*. Gaunt and Warren did four years together on TV in *No Place Like Home*. Diana Rigg and Denis Quilley have been an item in five separate productions: Macbeth and Lady Macbeth; Antony and Cleopatra; Agamemnon and Clytemnestra; the married couple in Agatha Christie's *Evil Under the Sun*; and a couple that were engaged in the film *In the House of Brede*. This would be their sixth time as a couple – that didn't include Quilley appearing in an episode of *The Avengers*. Meanwhile William Gaunt and Quilley last appeared together in *Noel's House Party* and Gaunt and Rigg had been at the same school at exactly the same time, Fulneck in Yorkshire, only the boys were kept in one building and the girls in another.

There were new combinations too: the mother-son relationship would bring together two actors from different generations both known for their acid intelligence. Three floors above, in the box office department, a woman was processing the returns from the priority booking forms that had been sent out earlier in the month. The mailing list brochure had carried an enticing photograph of Diana Rigg and Simon Russell Beale. It was a sepia picture of their two faces – a montage – with Rigg's face looking straight out and Russell Beale's face turned at 45 degrees. It was eery: the faces were so close that their cheeks might have been touching and yet they were unaware of one another.

This was a new play by a relatively unknown playwright but the response to the brochure had been *fantastic*. It was already clear that a great many people would be unable to get tickets to see the actors sitting round these four tables.

Simon Russell Beale was playing Felix Humble. Diana Rigg was playing his mother, Flora Humble. William Gaunt was playing the gardener, Jim. Denis Quilley was playing Flora's boyfriend, George Pye. Cathryn Bradshaw was playing George's daughter, Rosie Pye, who had once gone out with Felix. Marcia Warren was playing Mercy Lott, the neighbour, who pops round to lend a helping hand.

John Caird creased back the first page of the script and read the stage directions:
"Act One Scene One. Set. A pretty country garden ..."

William Gaunt

A PRETTY country garden... that had been the very first thought. Charlotte Jones had wanted to write a pastoral play with only one set. Her play *In Flame* had been a headache to write as it had lots of locations and time shifts. After that, she had written *Martha, Josie and the Chinese Elvis* which had only one set and that was... liberating. This new play was going to take place in the sort of English garden people remembered from childhood.

Then Charlotte Jones was talking to a friend who told her about a guy who had been at Oxford – a very good-looking guy, directed plays, got a first in English – your typical golden boy. In his late-20s he began to think God was telling him to kill himself and eventually he did try. He went back to live with his parents and worked two hours a week at the local charity shop. He was suffering from schizophrenia. Charlotte Jones was fascinated to know if this man was aware of what he had lost. Her friend was in no doubt about this: he was totally aware.

This second idea slotted in neatly with the first one: a golden boy – his name is Felix – comes back to the garden of childhood, where he bumbles around, unable to take off... and wasn't it true, or it may just have been apocryphal, that according to the laws of physics and aerodynamics, bumblebees weren't supposed to be able to fly?... perfect... bees would be an image running through the play... and at the end Felix would have to die, and it would be one of those *Thelma and Louise* climaxes, when the character jumps, leaps... flies.

Felix would be about 35 and he would be a student... except what could he be studying at 35 that would not leave the audience thinking, *If this guy's so brilliant how come he's still a student*? Around this time, early last year, the mathematician and physicist Brian Greene, author of *The Elegant Universe*, was on the radio talking in a very exciting, youthful – almost funky – way about superstring theory, hidden dimensions and the quest for the ultimate theory... and not long after the broadcast Felix became an astrophysicist and his special subject became unified field theory. This is the theory that attempts to bring together quantum mechanics and general relativity, the laws about the small things and the laws about the big things. It aims to come up with a perfect elegant supersymmetry: a quantum theory of gravity. As a small boy Felix had watched one of the Apollo moon landings and seen his father cry... he would be very emotional about science.

Gardens, golden boys, bumblebees, astrophysics... there was another big subject that appealed to Charlotte Jones... mothers and sons... the only drawback was that a play about a mother and son, with the son coming home from university and moping round the house in a gloomy suicidal sort of way sounded awfully like the plot of *Hamlet*... unless... unless the play embraced the idea of *Hamlet* and used the parallels to some effect. One of the characters could be a Polonius, another a Claudius: they wouldn't be exact, these similarities, but they would add resonance.

The central area of dramatic interest would be: *what's wrong with Felix?* But the question itself was shifting away from schizophrenia or severe depression, the sort of problems that might set members of the audience thinking about whether Felix was seeing the right consultant or taking the right medication. Felix's problem was moving closer to a state – the kind of *emotionally altered* state – that stems from grief. This was good news. *Humble Boy* was never going to be a play about medical issues. The plot of *Hamlet* also suggested the idea of a relationship between a son and his dead father. Into a pretty country garden in the Cotswolds stepped the figure of a ghost.

Denis Quilley

JOHN CAIRD continued, "The suggestion of an apple-tree, perhaps just some overhanging branches with a few apples." He read the description of Felix, *overweight but not unattractive*, who enters wearing cricket whites, and the neighbour, Mercy, *petite and timid*, who enters wearing black clothes and brown shoes. Simon Russell Beale and Marcia Warren went through their first scene, where they talk about the four beekeepers who have just removed the bees that Felix's father used to keep in the hive at the end of the garden. Flora enters, *a very attractive woman in her late 50s*. In an understated voice, Diana Rigg delivered her first full line, "I am not angry, Felix. I am incandescent with rage."

"Very good," said Caird, "Let's stop there for a minute." Pause. "Something that interests me about this..."

The next two and a half days proceeded along roughly these lines. The cast read a few pages of the play and John Caird hit the pause button. Sometimes the something that interested him was quickly answered, but often it wasn't, and those were usually the good ones: "If that's the case," he said, twitching his nose with amusement, "that opens a really good can of worms." Each query led to anecdotes, personal revelations and stories about families, friends and other actors. Little revelations led to larger ones and at any moment one of them might prove to be useful. Diana Rigg wondered about the bruising that occurred after a nose job. A member of the company was knowledgeable on the subject. When the nose was healing, it had to have bits of string dangling from the nostrils. Diana Rigg said: "That's my entrance." When any subject looked as if it was petering out, John Caird said: "Good. Let's read on."

It was pleasant enough if you weren't the writer. After lunch Charlotte Jones sat in a white plastic bucket seat, it wobbled and nearly turned over. "Why do I have to get the comedy seat!" she cried. Another seat was found but everyone knew that wherever she sat over the next three days it would always be the hot seat. Charlotte Jones hadn't been expecting to sleep during the first week: it was a gruelling time for an up-and-coming playwright to have actors of this calibre asking question after question after question. But if there was one situation that was worse than actors asking questions it was actors making suggestions: it wasn't bolshieness on her part, it was a sense of the precariousness of plays, one change that was agreed to in an unguarded moment might necessitate dozens of other changes that had never been envisaged, and in no time the house of cards would tumble down.

Anyone sitting round the table could gauge the size of the problems that were raised by following Charlotte Jones' left hand. If her hand tugged at a strand of hair and twisted it round her index finger this was a problem that would shortly be solved. If her hand swung up to her forehead and the tips of five fingers shielded her eyes, this was a problem that she might need to take back to Putney.

The truth is that even in the best-run rehearsal room there is no suggestion that can be made about a new script that does not touch a nerve. When Russell Beale made a comment to Charlotte Jones about a line in the play he held her hand for the duration of the comment and hugged her when he had completed it. Not even the politest man in the National Theatre – it is a feat to be able to walk through a door behind Russell Beale, he is always the one holding it open – not even Russell Beale could nuance the fact that he found four particular words in the script *impossible to stress*. It is a cliché that a playwright is like the parent of a newborn baby but in both cases the only remarks from other people that will suffice are expressions of enthusiasm. Everyone instinctively knew this in Rehearsal Room 3, it had been sucked dry of combativeness, grandstanding, point-scoring or machismo... the room was awash with consideration... which was why the favoured preamble, when raising a question about the script, was *Sorry, I'm being very thick about this ....*

Nevertheless! there were hundreds of questions about the script. Some of these were factual... *I'm sorry... I'm sorry...* but would you really use chilli in gazpacho soup?... wouldn't a better comic ingredient be pimentos?... *I'm sorry... I'm sorry...* but spaniels don't lure fowl to the water... spaniels *drive* fowl *off* the water... *I'm sorry...* but what type of rose *is* a Josephine Bruce?... no-one knew. Charlotte Jones had simply liked the sound of the name. There was an American ambassador called Bruce. Perhaps Josephine was the name of his wife. Marcia Warren and William Gaunt are gardeners with books on roses and the next day they reported, independently, that a Josephine Bruce is darkish-crimson, fragrant, high-centred and prone to mildew. The phrase *darkish-crimson* went into the script.

Some questions were speculative. Has Flora had other affairs? How many times, if at all, has Felix had sex in the last seven years? Some questions were about chronology. When X is in the garden, where is Y? Some questions were about motive. Why is Felix wearing cricket whites? Why has Flora had a nose job as opposed to a nip and a tuck? Why has Flora decided to have a nose job at this stage of her life? These questions were fun to pursue. And then, suddenly, Marcia Warren, asked, "Charlotte, why does Felix want to commit suicide?" Charlotte Jones hesitated, "I'm not sure I want to say. That maybe something that Simon wants to discover for himself." Caird and Russell Beale urged her to go on. Charlotte Jones spoke about Felix's relationship with his mother, with his ex-girlfriend, Rosie, and the stage he had reached in his research in astrophysics.

It was an act of faith. The actors, the writer and the director were talking about these events as if they had actually happened. Charlotte Jones could answer a question about why so-and-so did such-and-such by saying "there *was* a reason, but I can't remember it " and that was OK too. Sometimes the cast talked about the characters as if they were gossiping about colleagues they all knew. Sometimes the cast asked Charlotte Jones about her characters as if they were about to be introduced to strangers. On one point etiquette was strict. It was not on to refer to the character by the name of the actor playing that character: Diana Rigg does not enter the garden, *Flora* enters the garden.

To the outsider there is something faintly loopy about sitting around discussing the past sex lives of imaginary characters. It is like dropping in on some role-playing game in cyberspace and – in a similar way – the longer you hang around, and the more you buy into the exercise, the more powerful the experience becomes. Over two and a half days the minds of those around the table drew closer and closer as they strove to be shrewd and practical about lives that had never before been presented on stage.

FOR THE FIRST fortnight three members of the cast were performing in *Hamlet* and rehearsals started at 11am and finished at 5pm. With or without *Hamlet*, it was hard to imagine rehearsals lasting any longer. John Caird believes a company should have a life outside the rehearsal room. As soon as the day is over he heads for the exit. One morning he said, "I come to rehearsals to find calm." Simon Russell Beale knew what he meant: the other evening he had spent an hour trying to organise tickets for friends to see *Hamlet* and a little later in the evening when he walked on to the Olivier stage as Hamlet he thought... *here I can find calm...*

At the end of the first week John Caird picked up his car keys and battered black briefcase and went over to Charlotte Jones to say *see you Monday*. Charlotte Jones said, "I found this week quite hard. I felt it was going to be like dominoes. That one change would affect all the others." John Caird said that all the changes had been about clarifying the text, *why is... what is... how is...* ? "In a couple of weeks' time," he assured her, "the actors won't be letting you change a word. They'll know their characters better than you."

It was the morning of the third day that was the toughest. *Humble Boy* contains a wealth of themes, ideas and allusions that is filtered through the domestic story of two families. Its resolution was always going to be tricky. The cast read the final pages and the discussion that followed was about how and when to end the play. There were those who believed in an early ending, those who believed in a quiet ending and those who believed in a big ending. When Charlotte Jones had been writing *Humble Boy* she had fallen too much in love with the character of Felix to give him the *Thelma and Louise* treatment... slamming his foot down on the accelerator and driving over a cliff. At the close of the play Felix is about to drive back to Cambridge. On the final page and a half he opens the earthenware pot which contains his father's ashes and, in the presence of his mother, he scatters the ashes, releasing them to "the land of milk and honey". Flora says, "I'll leave you in peace then" and exits. The music grows, the beehive lights up like a rocket. Felix puts on his father's beekeeper hat and says "let be, let be". As he walks to the beehive we hear the NASA countdown, louder music and the swarm of bees.

Diana Rigg said, "I wonder if there could be a little bit of the old Flora in her final line so that it doesn't die away with 'I'll leave you in peace then.'"

There was no shortage of ideas for Diana Rigg's exit line. *Have you got petrol? Do you need a sandwich? Drive carefully.* Charlotte Jones said, *I won't wave* and later rewrote it as *Don't expect me to wave you off.*

John Caird wanted a quiet ending. He said that the emotional climax had been achieved with "extreme simplicity". There was a risk that the beekeeper's hat would look comical or might connect in the audience's mind with the thought that perhaps Felix had been about to commit suicide.

Charlotte Jones wanted a big ending. "I don't want it to become bathetic." (That's *bathos,* as in *anti-climax*.)

William Gaunt wanted an early ending. He said the play should end with the words *the land of milk and honey* and the scattering of the ashes: "but then that's because the play is all about me." But ending at *milk and honey* would deprive Felix of an echo from *Hamlet*. Charlotte Jones said, "I've got to have *let be, let be*."

The beekeeping hat served as a visual pun with the idea of the astronaut getting into the rocket. Outer space had joined bees as one of the strands of imagery running through the play. But the idea of a man going to the moon worried John Caird. "Felix's story is that he's finally come down to earth."

Charlotte Jones tossed her script on to the table and cried: "I'm going to lose my NASA moment!" Her tone was pitched half-way between playful indignation and genuine frustration. "All that metaphor, gone for nothing!"

The debate between EarlyEnders, QuietEnders and BigEnders went unresolved, rewrites were promised, more discussion was inevitable. The read-through was over.

"After lunch we'd better get on our feet," said John Caird. "Only for five minutes and then we can sit down again."

"Was I narky?" asked Charlotte Jones, during the lunch break. (That's *narky,* as in *sounding pissed off*.) "It's just it's not as if I haven't spent two and a half years thinking about all this."

THE STAGE MANAGERS cleared the four tables from the centre and counted out the metres as they laid down strips of electrician's tape to mark the boundaries of the garden. Simon Russell Beale has the first entrance, as Felix enters in his cricket whites. Russell Beale wanted shoes that were a size too big, those shoes from the 70s that were known as *cornish pasties*. When he entered he looked as if he was about to sink into the floor, like John Mills shuffling through the snow in *Scott of the Antarctic*. He trudged to the back of the rehearsal room and stared at a pile of cushions. The cushions represented the beehive. Felix's mother had instructed the beekeepers to take away the bees. The neighbour, Mercy, enters in black dress and brown shoes. Mercy has been sent out to the garden by Flora to bring Felix back into the house. Felix sees her and says "The b – b – b – bees have gone."

Felix asks Mercy what the collective noun might be for a group of beekeepers. Russell Beale twiddled a pen-knife in his hand as a displacement activity. "The more dysfunctional he appears at the beginning," said John Caird, "the greater the journey." Russell Beale made Felix's anger look infantile. Marcia Warren gave Mercy a quavery apprehensiveness: she was caught between Flora's orders in the house and Felix's questions in the garden. The angrier that Russell Beale became, the funnier it was to witness Marcia Warren's anxiety to please. "Good," said Caird and reminded them that they were standing in a garden. "You'll have to have slightly more *outdoor* voices."

Three pages in, Flora enters, wearing a navy blue dress designed by Jean Muir. Her late-husband's friends have come back to the house after the funeral. Diana Rigg said, "I wonder if I come in with a drink." John Caird thought that was a good idea. Rigg said, "She's military. It would definitely be a gin and tonic." Caird agreed, "Glasses of wine for everyone else and she's made herself a G & T." Rigg said, "As long as it doesn't look like water." A note was made for a tumbler, lemon and ice cubes. The cubes were transparent plastic and would never melt.

Mercy finds herself stuck between the mother and the son. Diana Rigg stood behind the bench at one end, Russell Beale sat on the steps at the other end. It is a tense moment. Felix had walked out of his father's funeral. Mercy reassures Felix that Flora isn't angry with him. Rigg sipped her imaginary G & T and said "I am not angry, Felix. I am incandescent with rage." After the line, there was a glimpse of her teeth and her tongue clung to her upper lip. *Incandescent* is a word that was tailor-made for Rigg, with its suggestion of glitter on the one hand and a furnace on the other. By the third week, when Rigg had put down her ringbinder folder, taken off her reading glasses, and was letting rip, it was only a little fanciful to think that Lady Macbeth or Clytemnestra had strolled into a pretty garden in the Cotswolds and was sipping a gin and tonic. In the seconds after *incandescent with rage*, Rigg's eyelashes went blink, blink, blink. The tilt of her chin said, *You have no idea the thoughts I'm holding back.*

Felix was transformed by Flora's presence. His stammer overwhelmed him. When Russell Beale stammered he would sigh before he attempted a new word and when he ran into a persistent stammer he clicked his fingers violently. The voice coach at the National, Patsy Rodenburg, had come into rehearsals and said *all stammers – unless they're pathological – start with the breath*. This is why stammerers sigh. The sigh is a way of breathing out in order to allow a new breath to come in, so that the stammerer can have another go. Rodenburg said that stammerers are predominantly middle-class and male and from families that are high achievers. (In Britain, stammering is rising rapidly within the Asian community.)

Why has Flora come into the garden? Mercy's task had been to bring Felix back. John Caird said, "Flora's come to find out what's happened to the messenger." And why do Flora and Felix end up having the argument? Diana Rigg said, "It's the stammering that just gets to her." Flora remarks on Felix's cricket whites, saying he was a "horror" at games. Caird suggested that Flora had been to Felix's prep school and seen how useless her son was at games. The next time Rigg uttered the word it had grown into "H-O-R-R-O-R" and those in the rehearsal room had a glimpse of the humiliating scene at that sports day 25 years before.

The tone of the scene changes as her anger turns to pain. "I've been missing the importance of three words," said John Caird, "*You weren't here.*" These are Flora's words to Felix. When her husband had died, Flora had to cope on her own. Felix has only just arrived from Cambridge. Diana Rigg sat on a wooden garden chair and the candour that she revealed in Flora at this moment drew Russell Beale towards her. Caird said to Rigg, "You stay where you are and he gets wooed towards you." Russell Beale said, "Black hole time."

Flora says that she couldn't bear to have her husband's belongings around the house. Felix makes an elliptical remark, "Just because you can't see something doesn't mean that it isn't there." Flora doesn't understand what he's saying, so Felix elaborates by talking about black holes, objects of infinite density and sophisticated micro-lensing techniques. In the context, it is a stupid remark. The moment of intimacy between mother and son has gone.

"This is the opportunity we have," said John Caird, "right at the top of the play, to suggest real closeness between them. So the audience can feel we've got to get them back together."

The rehearsal ended and the company headed towards the coffee, tea and biscuits.

"Could we have an upright chair?" asked Diana Rigg as she rose from her chair by the garden table, "Flora wouldn't slouch in a Jean Muir, and it's difficult not to slouch in that."

Marcia Warren

CHARLOTTE JONES doesn't want this to be *The Sixth Sense*, where a single shock in the narrative becomes the main talking point, but if you read the script you may easily reach the final pages before you realise that the gardener is the ghost: the gardener is Felix's father: Jim is James. It's possible that a member of the audience might spot the connection within the first 10 minutes. At this point in rehearsals, no-one knew what the audience would know or when they would know it. The James/Jim moments might be so obvious that the audience would click from the moment Jim enters and talks about floribundas and hybrids. Or the play might wrong-foot the audience for an hour and a half and they might experience a dawning realisation... an omigod... the gardener is the father!

The first meeting between Jim and Felix is a two-page scene that follows Flora's exit. Jim appears and apologises for turning up today but the garden is getting out of hand. He points out a darkish-crimson rose, a Josephine Bruce. They talk about the beekeepers taking away the bees. Jim says that some bumblebees have made a nest underneath the shed, but they'll only last the summer. Jim says Felix better go inside and see the guests.

Simon Russell Beale and William Gaunt ran the scene. As soon as it was over, Charlotte Jones imitated the deadpan reaction of an audience, "That'll be the dead father then."

William Gaunt said, "I've got to play the dead father."

As an actor he can only be truthful to the character he is playing. He can't deliberately deceive the audience. Of course he can do things that won't give the game away but it isn't his job to steer the audience into thinking that he isn't who he is.

John Caird said "It isn't your job as an actor. It's my job as a director."

The two identities of father and gardener aren't mutually exclusive. The father is a gardener. The difficulty arises when there are two actors on stage and their relationship is that of father and son. The audience will pick up on something – an intonation, a responsiveness, a depth of feeling – that wouldn't ordinarily exist between an astrophysicist and his parents' gardener.

John Caird said, "I shouldn't have cast good actors. If we didn't have good actors there wouldn't be a problem."

After the first rehearsal of this scene Charlotte Jones said that a friend of hers had visited the National Theatre's website and seen that someone had e-mailed asking if *Humble Boy* "derives" from *Hamlet*. The National had responded by saying that the play didn't *derive* from *Hamlet* but there were conscious echoes... *there is a ghost of his father.*

John Caird groaned and said, "Hel-lo?"

Cathryn Bradshaw

EVERY DAY in Rehearsal Room 3 there was the comforting illusion of progress. Every day a new part of the stage or a new piece of furniture arrived and if the right bit wasn't available, there was something else that stood in for it. Low wooden posts had been placed around the perimeter of the garden to indicate the height of the grass. To complete the effect, string was hung from post to post and from these pieces of string other pieces of string dangled to the ground. On one post, a large pink rose – a fake one – had been attached with an elastic band. It had a long stem, leaves, and three other small buds. This was the rose which George Pye gives to Flora in their first scene together: Scene Two. George has been having an affair with Flora and now that Flora's husband is dead, and it's a fortnight after the funeral, he has turned up to propose.

George enters the garden. He is *a beefy well-built man of about 60*. George is a Glenn Miller fan and wears his headphones as he listens to 'In The Mood'. The first time that Denis Quilley read this scene, sitting round the four tables in the centre of the room, he hummed the intro as well as the tune, cupped his hands round his ears to mime the headphones, swung from side to side in his seat, slammed out the percussion section with the palms of his hands, kicked one foot high above the table, went *glug-glug-glug* as he poured out the Pimms and cried "bugger" as he picked a rose and a thorn pricked his finger. Some actors take the first reading quietly. Quilley's would have gone down fine on the stage of Drury Lane, where he played the title role in *Sweeney Todd*.

The bright blue t-shirt, the tan, the beaming smile... it was positively *Caribbean*. Quilley referred to George as 'gin & Jag' and imagined he was a dab hand at the barbecues. William Gaunt noted that Quilley's accent as George was "a bit Estuary" which was good as Gaunt was going to "go for" south Yorkshire. Quilley's improvised reading charmed the whole table and it was a shame to think there would be a real jug, real headphones and a real (fake) rose, but here it was...

George enters, humming and carrying the Pimms. He picks the rose and places it behind the seat. When 'In The Mood' reaches the saxophone solo, Flora enters. They dance, he gives her a drink and, a little later, he gives her a ring and, a little later, he gives her the rose. Felix enters just in time to see George give Flora the rose. Flora tries to smell the rose but can't smell anything and – in a stage direction that gives the scene an unexpected twist – Flora hands the rose back to George to see if he can smell its scent. Caird spotted the possibility: in a non-naturalistic play, where there are few props, *a single one can take on enormous significance.* There are three main props in *Humble Boy*: the earthenware pot that contains the late James Humble's ashes; the garden hose that Felix wraps around his neck; and the rose. What marks these three out from the wine bottles, plates, secateurs, seedlings, pots, ashtray, napkins, lipstick, suncream, powder compact, headphones and torch is that they carry an emotional charge that increases in value.

"The rose can be a token running all the way through." said John Caird, "It could be that he holds the rose right through to the end."

In the dialogue that follows, Felix mocks the slogan that George dreamt up for his coach company and George mistakes astronomy for astrology. As Felix taunts his mother and her suitor, Quilley has to stand there twiddling the large pink rose with the three small buds, a garish symbol of everything he wants. As the rose rotates – back and forth, back and forth – it provokes Felix, embarrasses Flora and humiliates George. (There's a class dimension to all this: the Humbles are slightly grander than the Pyes.) You would never know, from reading the script, how the rose gathers momentum. It holds its own in rehearsals with Rigg, Quilley and Russell Beale. When George gives Felix a piece of his mind – "I don't give a shit if you piss your life away" – everything that George says is undermined by the ridiculous rose he has in his hand. It had become the fourth character.

Diana Rigg

AFTER SEVEN YEARS Felix has his first meeting with his ex-girlfriend Rosie. When Simon Russell Beale and Cathryn Bradshaw rehearsed this meeting (in Scene Four) no-one spoke a line from the script, or stood up, or moved from A to B, or thought about what to do with a prop. The afternoon was spent with John Caird and Charlotte Jones, sitting round the small white garden table, discussing a relationship that had taken place seven years ago. To help them understand the scene they were going to do they conjured up another scene that wasn't in the play. It was a world of probablys.

Felix probably came back to the Cotswolds for the summer and bumped into Rosie again. He had probably known her on and off for years. Cathryn Bradshaw had the strong feeling that Rosie had done *a lot of the work* – and, late in the summer, they probably had a sudden fling. Felix went back to his single bed in Cambridge, with the shared bathroom down the corridor, and Rosie probably went up to see him, and they probably went to a pub in Granchester and ate chicken in a basket and Felix probably took Rosie punting, which he couldn't get the hang of... and they probably had a drink with Felix's astrophysicist friends and Rosie probably embarrassed Felix by reminding him that he had said that if he ever discovered a star he would name it after her... *Rosie's star* –

– and the astrophysicists probably ignored her, because if someone doesn't know a lot about astrophysics, it's very hard to explain what exactly it is that you do – where would you begin?... with the idea that time isn't linear... that time travels faster at the top of a building than it does at the bottom... that the universe, which incidentally is 12 billion years old, may have as a many as 11 dimensions... that a light you see in the night sky left its source two million years ago... that anti-matter was discovered by working out a mathematical equation and believing that if the equation was right the proof would follow... most people don't even think about light in terms of *waves* –

– so when the astrophysicists in the pub remembered that Rosie was sitting next to them, they probably said *sorry where are you*? and she couldn't work out what they meant until someone else said *Girton? Newnham? Robinson?* No, no, she wasn't at the university, she lived in the Cotswolds, she was just here for the weekend, the only time she would be here for the weekend –
– and the *probablys* ran through the afternoon as writer, director and actors

considered when Felix and Rosie first had sex, and how often they had sex, and whether this was this was the first time for him (yes), and whether it was the first time for her (no), and how it had been (short and fierce), and whether he was searching for something maternal in sex (probably), and whether the first time Felix made love he burst into tears –

– and here they were, seven years later, with Rosie walking into the garden carrying a crash helmet. The crash helmet was an idea that came out of a costume discussion. These discussions were always held in the rehearsal room. John Caird said *all talk about costume is talk about character*. He thought Rosie might have green hair, something individual. The costume designer said Rosie might have walked into an antique shop and seen a divine jacket that was hanging at the back and it was her style and it was for sale. Caird said that they should try and imagine what Rosie did in her spare time (she works as a nurse)... someone suggested that Rosie had a motorbike, with a sidecar for her seven year old daughter... *that was good...* a crash helmet would be interesting –

Rosie enters the garden with a crash helmet... *early 30s, healthy-looking but quite plain...* and walks up to the beehive. Felix enters, wearing a sunhat. Rosie calls out to him, he is completely startled and repeats her name three times. Russell Beale delivered the line as a hyphenate: Rosie-Rosie-Rosie. Rosie replies, "Well, that's a good start then."

John Caird said, "What does *that's-a-good-start-then* mean?"

Charlotte Jones said, "Good, you can remember my name."

John Caird said, "I'm not sure that's clear."

Charlotte Jones said, "I imagined the rhythm of the Rosies would be spaced out."

John Caird said, "Rosie, pause, Rosie, pause, Rosie, pause."

The next time Russell Beale put in the three pauses and Cathryn Bradshaw moved down towards him.

John Caird said, "Go down the other way, then he can meet you on the diagonal." Cathryn Bradshaw walked down the steps and crossed the patio to the garden table. She went up to Russell Beale and pretended to slap him. Caird said, “This is a perfect place for a slap because there are only 10 members of the audience on the slap side. You're a right-hander, aren't you?” Bradshaw said, “Actually, I'm ambi – .” Caird said, “You beat men up with both hands.”

The fight consultant Terry King turned up to choreograph the slap. He told Cathryn Bradshaw to swipe the air about six inches away from Russell Beale's face. He explained to Russell Beale that when someone hits you in the face your hands fly up to your face. Terry King clapped his hands and covered his face. He recommended that Russell Beale turn at the same time. Things to remember: *don't be stationary. Don't try and disguise anything. What disguises the action is what you do afterwards not what you do before.*

Felix is carrying the earthenware pot with his father's ashes and Rosie asks Felix to put the pot down. Cathryn Bradshaw moved the pot out of the way and slapped him. She said to Russell Beale “As soon as I move the pot, you know I'm going to do it.” John Caird said, “Don't move the pot, because the audience might think the slap is something to do with the pot.”

After the slap, Rosie asks Felix to take off his hat. She looks at him and says “that's good”, she is not in love with him any more. The actors were thinking about the emotional relationship, the director was thinking about the spatial one. The scene was static. John Caird said, “Cathy, you've been in this relationship for half a page. If you go walkies on *I'm-not-in-love* to about here... ” He walked towards the bench, “This is a good spot”. He went back to his seat by the stage managers. “That's my best shot. I've directed the hell out of that.”

In one of the breaks the cast had been talking about the sounds people make when they have orgasms and how important it is for actors to have another repertoire of sounds that they can employ when they have to do sex scenes in front of the camera. *This is not the noise I actually make!* In the following section in this scene Rosie kisses Felix, thinks about having sex just-for-hell-of-it and reckons that it would be good for Felix too – she's a nurse, she knows what's best. Russell Beale was sitting on the sunlounger. Cathryn Bradshaw approached him in a mock-sexy way, pulled down his trousers and straddled him. Before the actors could do their versions of the sounds *they don't actually make*, there is the sound of a car pulling up outside. Felix and Rosie hurry into the long grass in a state of undress. Russell Beale said, “We need to make a costume note. My knickers will be visible.” The conversation turned to what colour underpants Felix would wear. Grey. Probably.

Simon Russell Beale, drawn in rehearsal by Andrew Tyzack

WHAT EXACTLY the audience thinks is happening, after it glimpses Felix's underpants, became the subject of a long discussion. One of the main jobs of a director is to control what an audience is thinking or feeling at any given moment. Scene Four takes place in the evening and within this scene there are a number of mini-scenes. It begins in the early evening, when Rosie enters with her crash helmet and Felix enters with his sunhat. It continues through to late evening, when Flora and George return home after a boozy dinner. It ends at night-time, when Jim appears with a torch. Scene Four is 12 pages long and spans about four hours. It takes place outdoors, in the height of summer.

In an outdoor scene a significant change of lighting usually registers with an audience as *time passing*. If a man and woman head off into the long grass and there is a change in the lighting, the audience will almost certainly think that the couple had sex during the lighting cue. It's a fast-forward. The lighting designer, Paul Pyant, would be joining them later. But there was a plot point to work out with the cast. John Caird said, "My question is, because Felix and Rosie have got to disappear, do we imagine that they've had sex, and if not, why not?"

Charlotte Jones said, "They shouldn't have sex."

John Caird said, "People will assume that Flora and George have come back a couple of hours later, and will assume that Felix and Rosie have been up there a long time, and it will be a bit post-coital."

At this point in rehearsals, John Caird was dividing the scene into separate periods in the evening, with lighting changes that suggested the passage of time in-between. Charlotte Jones said, "I really like real time." She didn't want any breaks or jumps.

John Caird said, "In that case we'll have to lose the sunhat. The trouble is, we're midsummer. So it will all have to be quite late."

Simon Russell Beale said, "The hat's no great loss compared to other potential losses."

Felix and Rosie would have to meet when it was dusk. So there was no need for Felix's sunhat. Russell Beale said that it would be perfectly in character for Felix to wear his sunhat even when there isn't any sun.

John Caird said, "The thing that's very difficult to do on stage is twilight."

On stage, twilight can look very close to interior lighting. The scene might lose its sense of taking place outdoors. A low light is never good in a play with funny lines as the facial reactions of the other actors to a line is as important as the line itself.

John Caird thought the scene could begin just as the sun was setting. He said, "We'll get away with some very low angle sunlight." The lighting changes that moved the play from dusk to late-evening would have to be almost imperceptible. "It has to be subtle so that it doesn't trigger the audience into thinking a scene change has happened, in which case they'll be triggered into thinking Felix and Rosie have had sex."

Felix and Rosie would meet at dusk and the light would continue to darken through their scene. When they are about to have sex they hear the sound of a car and they run up into the long grass by the beehive. George enters, almost immediately, and there is an opportunity for a lighting change. When George and Flora get back to the house Flora would switch on lights. John Caird said, "We'll have a crack of artificial light from the house, when George enters." With this rapid transition no-one in the audience should be able to think that Rosie and Felix have had sex. After George and Flora have gone back indoors, Rosie and Felix would talk, perhaps lit by the light from the house. After Rosie leaves, the lights from the house would need to go out. (Flora might have drawn the curtains.) Felix is alone and Jim enters. Caird said, "It has to be completely dark when Jim comes on with his torch."

John Caird would talk to the lighting designer, Paul Pyant. Simon Russell Beale and Cathryn Bradshaw prepared to make their entrances again. Diana Rigg and Denis Quilley sat behind tables waiting to make theirs. Caird said, "Let's go from the top again."

Charlotte Jones tapped her pencil on her desk in a mock-authoritarian manner and said, "And don't let us think that you've had sex or fallen asleep or any time has elapsed."

GEORGE AND FLORA intend to announce their engagement at a small lunch party in the garden. The whole of Act Two takes place on that one day. Felix and Rosie are attending the lunch and so is Mercy, who wasn't really invited. It's immediately obvious in the rehearsal room that, as an institution, meals weren't invented for the benefit of audiences. The best seat to have for watching a meal is a seat at the table. No actor wants to get stuck at the table with half the audience watching the back of his or her head, which is why there is always one character who is reluctant to join the table and another character who is bursting to get up and break away.

In *Humble Boy* Felix arrives late, wearing clothes that shock his mother. Earlier in rehearsals, John Caird had said, "Everyone at the party should be beautifully turned out so that when Felix enters –"

Charlotte Jones said, "Everyone except Mercy –"

John Caird said, "Mercy *thinks* she's beautifully turned out."

The lunch party scene runs from page 46 to page 87. John Caird said, "It's a long time for one costume. It might need variation."

Charlotte Jones suggested a pashmina for Flora.

Diana Rigg said, "Very good idea. As the afternoon passes, she can put it on."

When they rehearsed the scene, John Caird said, "It would be a strong statement if Flora sat at one end and George sat at the other." That might be where Flora would like George to sit, but it wasn't necessarily where the director wanted George to sit. Caird tapped the end of the table nearest the audience. "The ideal way to construct the meal for sightlines is not to have anyone sitting here."

Russell Beale pointed at the white garden table and said, "We could have the wine over there." Charlotte Jones said, "That's good." Russell Beale said, "To have the wine there releases Denis and me. You can get it for the ladies, Denis. I can get it for myself."

John Caird said, "Just for now, let's lay the plates, and the soup can go down in the middle."

Marcia Warren entered carrying a tray with a tureen. The tureen slid on the tray and the lid rattled. She placed it on the table and lifted off the lid. She looked at the soup, dipped her finger in it, and noticed the salt and pepper, added a bit of both, closed her eyes as she tasted it again, and looked to see what else she could add. There was an earthenware pot next to the salt and pepper, which had something spicy in it. She tasted it... *mmnn, nice...* she put some into the gazpacho and gave it a good stir. She tasted the gazpacho again... *better...* it still needed more. She sprinkled in lots of the spice, gave it another stir and tasted it again. *Perfect.*

Act Two opens with five of the characters about to sit down and consume the ashes of the sixth character. The gazpacho had now become a *ticking bomb* that the audience is waiting to see explode. Before that moment arrived, the cast of *Humble Boy* had to try and achieve something that looks very simple. Each person had to enter, sit down, pour themselves drinks or have one poured for them and wait, while Marcia Warren went round the table with the tureen and ladle dolloping some gazpacho on to each of their plates. The one other thing the cast had to remember to do was to say their lines. In short, they were entering *prop hell.*

All morning they sat at the table, going over it, and over it, and over it – *sorry, my fault! no, it was mine! can we do that again?* – until each individual action had found its place. This stage of rehearsals cannot be rushed. It goes at its own pace until every actor knows for sure how long it takes to pour the glass of wine, how much wine will be left in the bottle, when exactly they get up from the table and when exactly they go back to the table. Once the actors have this sequence fixed in their minds, they will be extremely reluctant to change it.

Marcia Warren went round the table with the tureen of soup, giving some to each character, and every time one of the cast made a mistake – *my fault! can we go back?* – she waited as a stage manager tipped the gazpacho out of the plates and back into the tureen and refilled the wine bottles. The rehearsal was disciplined, frustrating and often comic. Marcia Warren said, "It seems so simple when you serve soup at home."

Above: Trish Montemuro, John Caird, Simon Russell Beale, William Gaunt, ASM Andrew Speed, Diana Rigg, Denis Quilley and Marcia Warren

REHEARSAL PHOTOGRAPHS BY CATHERINE ASHMORE

Stage Manager Trish Montemuro and John Caird

Left, top: Simon Russell Beale and Diana Rigg

Left: William Gaunt

Above: Denis Quilley and Marcia Warren

Left, top: Cathryn Bradshaw, DSM Fiona Bardsley, and Charlotte Jones

Left: Simon Russell Beale

Above: Denis Quilley

$E = mc^2$
H He Li

Left: Simon Russell Beale

Above: William Gaunt

Above: Charlotte Jones

Right: Diana Rigg

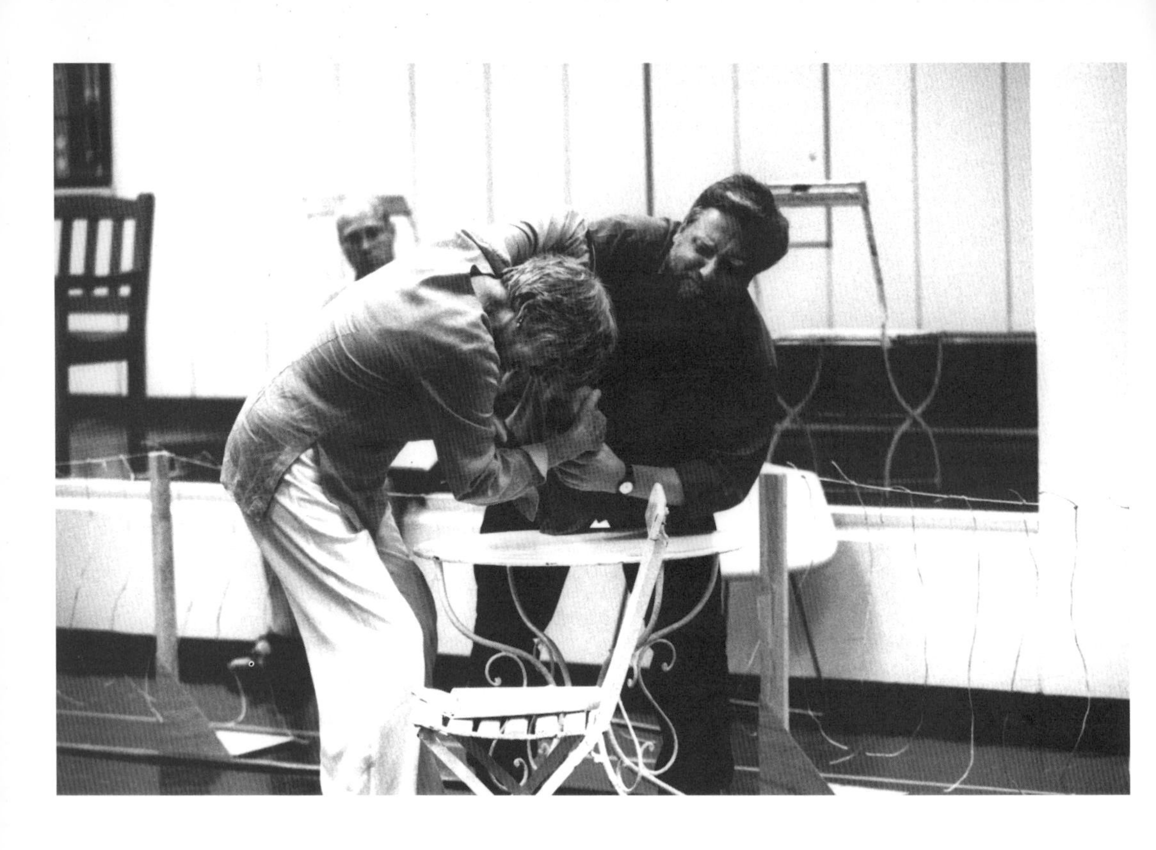

Above: Diana Rigg and Simon Russell Beale, with rehearsal artist Andrew Tyzack in the background

Above: Cathryn Bradshaw and Charlotte Jones

Top: Diana Rigg

Above: Marcia Warren

Above: Simon Russell Beale

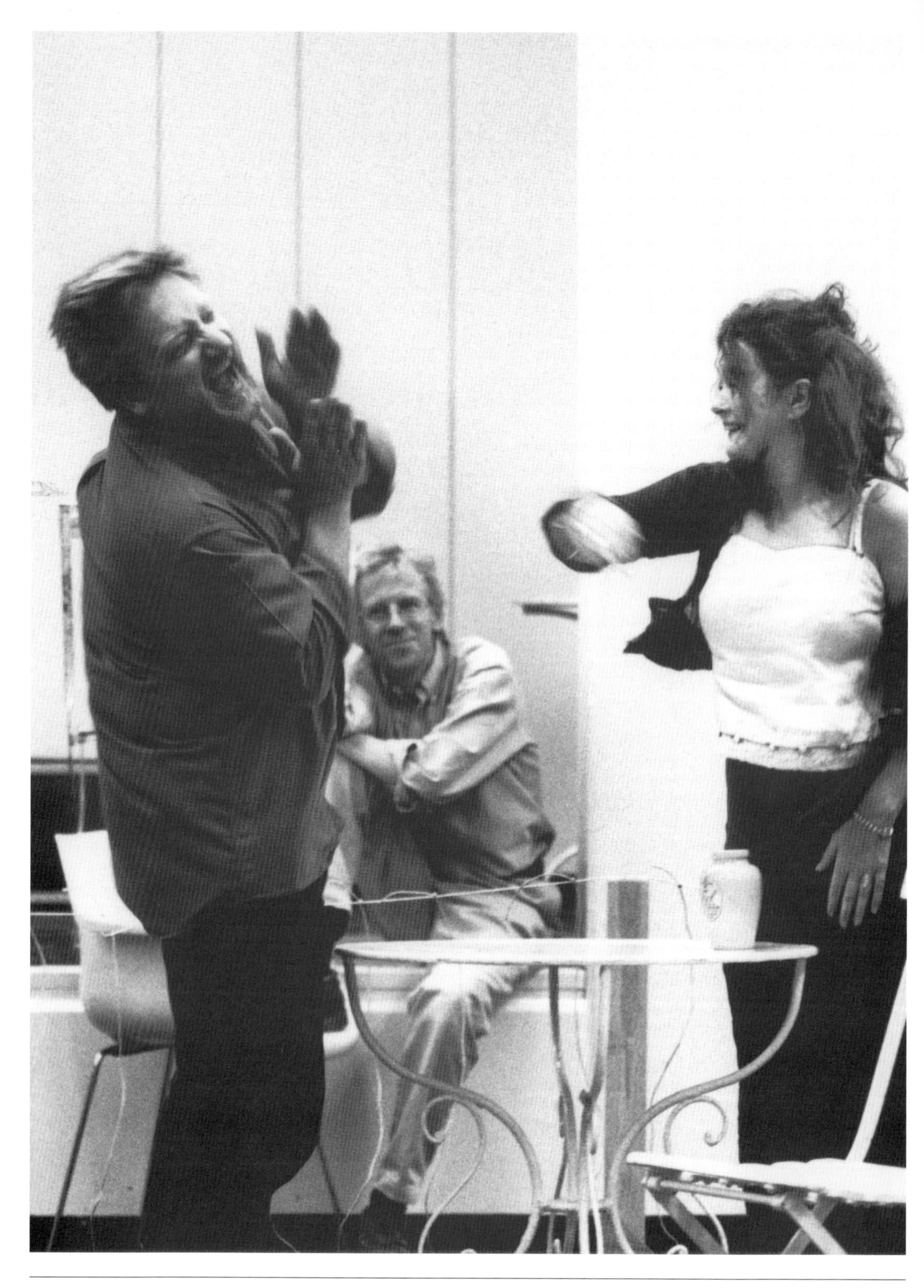

Above: Simon Russell Beale and Cathryn Bradshaw, observed by Robert Butler

Above: Diana Rigg

FLORA: ... It was stupid of me.

FELIX: No, no it wasn't stupid. But I'm not b-brave enough to let go.

FLORA: Thank God!

FELIX: B-b-but I still want – the p-p-p possibility – of another life – the p-possibility of other dimensions

Pause. Flora picks up the ashes, puts them down before him.

FLORA: Say the words.

He does not pick them up.

FLORA: You know them. You've always known them.

He picks them up.

FELIX: (with difficulty) The day that a man...

Top: Zoë Martlew (cellist), William Gaunt, and composer Joe Cutler

Above: A page from Charlotte Jones' re-writes during rehearsals

Top: John Caird and Marcia Warren

Above: Charlotte Jones

ON THE Friday of Week Four a newspaper on the stage manager's desk carried the headline *Archer jailed*. Next to the newspaper sat a copy of the production schedule for *Humble Boy*. The production manager, Di Willmott, had distributed this two-sheet schedule to about 30 people. It gave an hour-by-hour breakdown of the technical tasks that had to be accomplished. The author of two West End plays, Jeffrey Archer would be just completing his first fortnight in prison when *Humble Boy* had its first preview. The production schedule began at 09.00 on Monday July 30 with *commence fit-up, rig lx* (lx is lights) *and rig sound* and continued on Tuesday, with *commence band call*, and Wednesday, with *commence technical rehearsal*, and Thursday with *Lambeth licensing inspection*, right through to Friday August 3 with *commence dress rehearsal, half hour call* and – at 19.30 that evening – *preview 1*. First nights are always regarded as the major test of any production, but probably the scariest moment is the first time it is presented in front of an audience.

John Caird was keen to run the whole play at the end of Week Four. It would give him a strong idea of the priorities for the next week's rehearsals. The last scene hadn't been rehearsed in detail, but that was no problem, he assured the cast, they could run the play up to that point, and if the actors didn't want to do the final scene, they could stop there, and if they did want to do it, they could carry on to the end. (Before the run, the cast didn't want to do it; during the run, they did it.) The composer, sound designer, designer and costume designer came in to watch the run. Bits of costume were filtering into rehearsals. Some of the shoes had arrived. Simon Russell Beale had the brown ones, a size too big, with the stitching on the top, the cornish pasties. Marcia Warren had high heels with sparkly straps. Diana Rigg said, “If nothing else, the shoes will get a laugh.” Caird said, “Someone said if you get the shoes right everything else will follow.” Russell Beale said, “That was Beryl Reid.” Caird said, “Sometimes it's only the shoes that are right.”

William Gaunt had a pair of battered brown brogues. They were also a size too big, but he thought they had weathered in just the right way, so he would wear two pairs of socks. Gaunt didn't exactly enter and exit in these shoes, he drifted in and out, with the measured tread of someone immersed in his own world. Gaunt had to garden in a way that was convincing and earthy and yet wasn't at odds with the non-naturalism of the set. Each of Jim's entrances, until the final one, worked around a self-contained activity. He clipped with the shears or snipped with the secateurs or sprinkled tea-leaves over the roses or sipped a cup of tea or searched for slugs with his torch. When he stopped to wipe his silver hair back over his forehead or slip his secateurs into his back pocket, the message was, *no rush.*

The sound designer, Christopher Shutt, had given stage management a mini-disc with sound cues. These ranged from the horn from George's Jaguar, to birdsong in the Cotswolds, to the snatches of Glenn Miller that George plays on his Walkman. The birdsong contained a hundred separate bird noises or "twits", as Shutt calls them, including wrens, warblers and nightingales. In the evening scene naturalists in the audience would spot the sound of a tawny owl and a fox. The sound cue that preceded Cathryn Bradshaw's first entrance was the noise of the engine of a Honda 125 pulling up on the drive, idling for a few seconds and cutting out. In the run Bradshaw waited another second or two so the audience would know that she had parked the motorbike properly, otherwise they might be sitting there wondering if the next sound cue was going to be the noise of a motorbike crashing to the ground. Bradshaw entered in a leather jacket, carrying a crash helmet, a rucksack and a bunch of keys. That was the physical baggage. The emotional baggage took longer to reveal itself. Rosie has seven years of pent-up emotions: she was dumped by Felix and she has a lovely daughter, Felicity. Rosie isn't sure what she wants to reveal to Felix. In those fraught moments, Bradshaw tapped her keys grimly against her crash helmet and her eyes hid behind two strands of hair that curled down her face. Felicity is the most important off-stage character in the play. In some ways, the plot turns around her. In one of the most graphic gestures in the run, Russell Beale moved his palm up and down in the air as he tried to guess the height of a seven year old.

You could watch rehearsals for a month and then watch the first run and think where did that come from? Sometimes work done in rehearsals showed through, other times, what took place was new. In this first run Marcia Warren was blowing the fringe of hair off her forehead as the day was so hot. Diana Rigg was keeping her cigarette on the edge of her lips and letting it wag up and down, as she turned on Rosie with withering disdain and said: "If we want a Nurse Pye nugget, we'll ask for it"... Peter O'Toole used cigarettes to similarly withering effect in *Jeffrey Bernard is Unwell.* When Flora orders Mercy to go away, the palms of Rigg's hands were waving in front of her hips like the lady of the manor shoo-ing a stray sheep out of the vegetable garden. Russell Beale was turning his right leg on the ball of his foot – in and out, in and out – like a schoolboy. William Gaunt was walking down from the beehive to the patio when he stopped and stared at something very surprising that seemed to be happening on the rehearsal room wall... Jim had seen a floribunda that had just come out. When Gaunt was pointing out the flowers to Rigg, her eyes were filling with tears.

Caird sat between the stage managers' tables, a slim spectacled figure, tearing off pieces of electrician's tape and sticking each one onto the edge of a table in a patterned fan. His manner had changed from the unruffled amusement of the anchorman to the singular attentiveness of the umpire. One of the two assistant stage managers, or ASMs, Andrew Speed, said that after a couple of weeks in a rehearsal room nearly everyone loses objectivity. A production might be wonderful, a production might be awful: who knew? As Caird massaged the back of his head with his hand, it was tempting to place faith in the idea that he must know. One of his shows, *Les Misérables*, was playing all over the world. (He co-directed *Les Mis* and *Nicholas Nickleby* and *Peter Pan* with Trevor Nunn.) When the cast of *Hamlet* visited Boston the actors discovered that Caird had two other productions on in the city. He was even writing a book about directing. He had to know. After Act One, Caird said that there was one section that he had directed in the wrong way or *maldirected*. It was Flora and George's first scene when George proposes to Flora. Diana Rigg and Denis Quilley were picking up on each other's rhythms and intonations as if they were in love and their minds were at one. As Caird watched the run, he realised that in the play Flora was already moving on and, if only subconsciously, she knew her relationship with George was over.

All through the first run the deputy stage manager, or DSM, Fiona Bardsley, followed the script, reading out a line if it was omitted, and putting a pencil mark against a word if an actor got it wrong, and rubbing out a pencil mark if the actor had got a word wrong last time and had now got it right. From the first day of rehearsals, Bardsley had noted down each line change and on the opposite page each move that was made. Lighting, music and sound cues would also be marked in. During this first run an actor would suddenly speak a line that had no connection with the text... *now I've got a big speech, haven't I?... I say something, don't I?... yes?... yes?... help me!* Actors exited, returned to seats, put on reading glasses, checked lines. They had each learnt at their own pace. Russell Beale had always been the first into rehearsals, either running lines with one of the stage managers, or walking through a scene on his own. He learnt his lines as soon as possible. He found it reassuring that whatever else happened he would be able to go on and do it. "That's why I could never be a director," said Russell Beale, "You have to deal with everyone working at a different pace." Other actors preferred to learn the lines while they were on their feet. During rehearsals, Diana Rigg was always the first to break away from the discussions and say, *Okay, let's do that. Where shall we go from? Let's try it.* Marcia Warren used the technique of Pelmanism, a system of memory training. It was essential when each page of the script has about 25 lines of dialogue and your character has two lines on p51, and they were probably non-sequiturs, and two lines on p52, six lines on p53, one line on p54, four lines on p55, and three lines on p56. If one sentence contained the word "hole" and the next started with the word "So..." Marcia Warren remembered the cue by thinking that if there was a *hole* it would need *sewing*.

The first run gave the clearest idea of what type of play *Humble Boy* was: an ensemble piece in which every character is changed by the events in the play and every character gets to show contrasting sides of his or her personality. The first run revealed the sheer speed with which the play shifts moods as it switches from intimate moments to cruel ones or farcical ones. John Caird told the cast that they didn't have to go and find the characters, they had to let the characters come and find them. The times when the run hadn't worked was when he had lost sight of the actors as themselves. What he could see was the effort the actors were putting in to playing the characters. He said, "On Monday afternoon, let's run it again." Diana Rigg said, "I think so." Russell Beale said, "Good idea." Caird said, "It's so much to do with ensemble playing."

THE FIFTH week was spent fine-tuning... *there's a new impetus here... it needs to accelerate... there's a beat that's being missed... that pause rather lets the air out... the intention isn't quite clear... don't play that before it happens...* fixing little bits that didn't quite work or had never seemed right. It was the week of tweak.

And the artistic side, the growth of a performance, was inextricably connected to sorting out the most prosaic details. The vulgar cheeriness that George displays early on changes into a desperate sourness. The role was deepening with each run, but to watch Denis Quilley rehearse was to see him deal with practicality after practicality. He asked Cathryn Bradshaw to pick her wineglass up from the table and lift it towards him so that he would gain an extra second when he went round the table filling the three other glasses. On his final exit, Quilley has to fend off a bee. How do you fend off an imaginary bee on stage when the sound cue of a bee is on the speakers? The trick with bee-acting is that when the sound is loudest on the speakers, the bee is thought to be closest to the actor, which is when Quilley has to fend it away most violently. Sometimes exactness expressed itself through deliberate inexactness. Quilley volunteered to fix the moment when he ran back into the garden brandishing the garden hoe, but Diana Rigg said, "I'd like to be surprised every single night by different timing, otherwise it becomes a comedy routine." The props were becoming more precise too. Flora receives a letter from the Royal Entomological Society. The envelope that is used in the scene carried the franking stamp of that organisation. A memo from the ASM Valerie Fox said: *We are now using an oblong breadbasket in Act Two, and as Diana Rigg is the only one eating any bread she would like soft white rolls.*

If there was a film of the playwright-in-rehearsals it would have to be called *Charlotte Jones' Diary...* the camera would pan across the stage managers' desks, with the telephone, aspirins, scissors, chalk and highlighter pens... it would take in the blackboard on which an astrophysicist, who had come in one morning to give a talk, had chalked up equations and the names of two books he recommended, *The Elegant Universe* and Timothy Ferriss's *The Whole Shebang...* the camera would settle on a desk at the furthest end, littered with sheets of rewrites and a couple of M&S bags with apples or plums or cherries. It was the playwright's desk. Charlotte Jones sat there, with her sunglasses perched on her head, periodically lobbing remarks into the centre of the rehearsal room. By Week Five it was her turn to be picky. The final version of the text had been sent to her publishers, Faber & Faber, and that had only increased her reluctance to make any more changes. The camera would follow her as she rose from her desk and walked towards the tea urn, with its oddball collection of mugs, and the sign on the wall listing the prices and saying *please pay or face delay on future stocks!* The camera would close in on the biscuit tin: inside we would see rich teas *(bad),* chocolate digestives and bourbons *(v. bad)* and custard creams *(v. v. bad)*... but what other diversion was there for a playwright in Week Five!... the camera would then follow the playwright as she made the journey back – past the entire stage management team – to her desk. It would be a long tracking shot. It had been dubbed *the walk of shame.*

TURN LEFT outside the doors of Rehearsal Room 3, and you might find yourself wandering up a staircase, with dirty white walls and red railings and steps that smelt of disinfectant, and walking along a corridor of offices similar to that in any big corporation with noticeboards, conference rooms and internal banking facilities. Turn right outside the doors of Rehearsal Room 3, and you might find yourself walking along pea-green corridors, past actors' dressing rooms, with walls of old production photos, that included one of Marcia Warren in *Tons of Money* and one of Denis Quilley in the National's *Sweeney Todd.* Walk up another staircase, with dirty white walls, red railings and steps that smelt of disinfectant, and you might enter a room with four full-length mirrors attached to the wall. A rack of clothes stood against the wall with green plastic name tags that looked very familiar.

Pale green shirts and cords hung beneath the tag with the name "Jim"; a cream shirt and cream trousers and a navy blue dress hung beneath "Flora"; a pink print blouse and beige skirt hung beneath "Mercy"; a suede jacket, dyed skirt and embroidered shirts hung beneath "Rosie"; and beige chinos and a blazer hung beneath "George". The cricket whites that Felix wears had been thrown into a washing machine with a black sock to take the whiteness out. Pure white can distract on-stage and Felix was the sort of person who would mix his socks up with his cricket whites. On a desk near the clothes rack lay two pale blue cardigans from Jaeger. Diana Rigg might put on one of them as the evening turned cooler in Act Two. (The idea of the pashmina had been discarded.) In her first scene Flora enters wearing a Jean Muir dress and mentions the designer's name. To be strictly naturalistic, each character would possess half a dozen outfits and they would pick and choose whatever they felt in the mood to wear that day. But there wasn't the budget.

One floor above the costume rack there was a room with row upon row of washing machines and tumbledriers. Walk a little further on, past the Gerald Scarfe poster of Russell Beale in *Battle Royal,* and through a room with vats of dye, and you would reach a table that had Flora's wig sitting on it. The hair was coiled in red curlers, and was waiting to go into an oven. It was a Jackie Onassis-type wig. In the discusssions about what hair Flora might have, Diana Rigg had said, "Any ideas?" Her own hair in rehearsals was a shortish crop with shades of blonde. Charlotte Jones said, "I think your hair is a bit London." Rigg suggested a wig. John Caird wondered if Flora might be the sort of person who looks a bit different every time you see her. "No!" said Rigg, with the certainty of an actress who has got her character in her sights, "She has found her look!" Goldie Hawn and Joan Collins were examples of women who had found their look. Jackie O was another. "A bit bouffant," suggested Rigg, "The hair hardly moves. Hardly a hair out of place." Quilley and Russell Beale had started rehearsals with the beards they had in *Hamlet*. Both had shaved them off. Russell Beale had curls put in his hair which Felix would twiddle in moments of stress. Quilley thought George's hair would be smartly brushed. "Possibly a 'tache." Caird said that Quilley should keep his moustache. "There's something about a 'tache that says, *I'm at it*."

Marcia Warren would have her hair done during the interval so that when Mercy goes to the lunch party, to which she hasn't been invited, she has made an extra effort. Andrew Speed, the ASM, had already given the dressers, those responsible for getting the actors on stage in the right clothes, the provisional timings for the costume changes. Every primary entrance and final exit had been timed. Cathryn Bradshaw was the last on: she has 52 minutes to wait before her first entrance. Marcia Warren was the first off: she has 30 minutes in her dressing room before the curtain call. The publications department had been informed that the first act of *Humble Boy* ran one hour and 10 minutes and the second act ran 59 minutes. The programme would give the running time, which included the interval, as two hours 25 minutes. The company had spent 25 days rehearsing a play that ran for 129 minutes. That worked out at five minutes a day or one minute an hour.

On the Friday afternoon of Week Five the results of the one-minute-an-hour rehearsals were presented to about 20 people from within the building, each of whom had some connection with the production. John Caird thanked those who were there for being the play's first audience. "Here we go then... music... which we don't have... house lights going down... which we don't have..."

Simon Russell Beale entered, wearing his cornish pasties.

THE MUSIC arrived on Monday in the shape of three musicians and one composer – or one piano, one cello and an alto and a soprano saxophone. The music presented a new prospect: the audience would leave the theatre humming three notes. The main theme that the composer Joe Cutler had written began with a crotchet, then dropped almost an octave to a quaver and then rose a tone to a second quaver. The effect is known as a *falling seventh.* Edward Elgar, the master of the elegiac touch, had been keen on them. A little arpeggio followed the three notes. For Joe Cutler, the first three notes expressed the pastoral quality of the play: its Englishness and its nostalgia. The little arpeggio, the run of ascending notes, was a musical version of Felix's struggle to take flight. The music that Cutler composed for *Humble Boy* also contained motifs for the bees, the tinnitus and a lazy English summer. John Caird had heard Cutler's music when he had gone to the Purcell Room on the South Bank earlier in the year. His nephew, Adam Caird, had been playing the piano and Adam's fiancée, Charlotte Bradburn, played the saxophone. John Caird had the idea, as he listened to Bradburn play in several of the pieces that evening, that the saxophone would be a very good instrument for doing the sound of the bees. When Caird heard Cutler's piece, which was titled 'Urban Myths', he spotted a composer with the right theatricality and humour to write music for the play. During the run of *Humble Boy*, Adam Caird would play the piano, Charlotte Bradburn the two saxophones, and Zoë Martlew the cello.

On Tuesday afternoon they ran the play with the music. Afterwards, Caird gathered the actors round the table and briefed them about the next few days. The stage management team pulled the electrician's tape off the floor and wound up the string that had enclosed the acting area, and the stage crew cleared away the rostra. The *mark-up*, the tape marking the stage area, is usually kept for understudy rehearsals, but there are no understudies at the Cottesloe. The audience is too small for it to be financially worthwhile.

Rehearsal Room 3 had been an almost hermetic world, in which a dozen people met each day to create a fictional world. But real life kept intruding: one member of the company had been in and out of hospital; another had got married; another was about to become a father again; and another – a sex symbol from the Sixties – had her 63rd birthday. An astrophysicist had come in to talk about the universe; a beekeeper had brought in his bees; there had been a picnic lunch with gazpacho from Moro and on Friday evenings there had been champagne cocktails. One member of the company remarked, with no sourness, that it was the worst rehearsal room in the world. Another said that under European Union regulations, livestock wouldn't be allowed to be kept in these conditions. The play had been rehearsed in a room with no windows and would be performed on a stage that pretended to be outdoors. Caird said the set was "about as different from this room as its possible to get." The next morning the company would meet on the stage of the Cottesloe. There would be two days of technical rehearsals and two dress rehearsals.

THREE DAYS later, on Friday August 3, Trish Montemuro sat in the Cottesloe dock, the area which linked the stage of the theatre to the maze of corridors that led to the dressing rooms. Around her stood bits of scenery and spare blocks of long grass, and above her hung two flags from earlier productions. Montemuro had been closely involved with this production since reading the third draft of the script on the American tour of *Hamlet*. After stage-managing the six weeks of rehearsals, this evening was the moment of changeover. Half an hour before the first performance, the production of *Humble Boy* officially became her responsibility. At 7.25pm, Montemuro switched on the microphone and spoke to the company, "Cottesloe Theatre, Cottesloe Theatre, ladies and gentlemen of the *Humble Boy* company, this is your Act One beginners' call. Stand by Miss Rigg, Miss Warren, Mr Gaunt, Mr Russell Beale. Stand by musicians, sound, lighting." The actors left their dressing rooms and assembled in the Cottesloe dock.

In the control box, at the back of the auditorium, the deputy stage manager, Fiona Bardsley, had headphones on, through which she could speak to lighting, sound, musicians, the stage management team and stage crew. Just after 7.30pm the Cottesloe's house manager gave Bardsley front-of-house clearance. The 300 people attending the first preview had all taken their seats in the auditorium. As John Caird liked to say: the seventh character had arrived. Charlotte Jones and her husband, Paul Bazely, were sitting in the centre of the stalls. The playwright had her arms folded and her legs crossed. Caird sat immediately behind and above them, on the first level, with his notebook open. Some members of this audience had spent a couple of hours queuing for tickets that had been returned to the box office at the last minute. Montemuro said, "Stand by everyone." Bardsley said, "Stand by sound cue one... stand by music cue one... stand by lx cue one..." Sound, music and lighting replied by pressing a cue light that flashed on her desk. Bardsley said, "Sound cue one and lx cue one... go." The house lights went down. Paul Bazely put his hand on his wife's knee. Over the last couple of years he had walked past his wife's desk in their flat in Putney and seen stacks of books - on the desk, on the floor around the desk – books on bees, books on astrophysics and, one day, a copy of *Hamlet*. At the time, he had asked, *What's this doing here?* In a few seconds time, an idea that had originated two and a half years ago – about a golden boy returning to the garden of his childhood – would encounter its first audience. The music began. There was the sound of bees buzzing. The lights came up on an English country garden.

The garden was *so* green. It was an explosion of grass dotted with wild flowers. The grass had arrived on the Monday when two lorries delivered dozens of blocks of tall reedy grass that stood in the sunshine next to the National's unloading bay. The high bank of grass had to be assembled like a 3-D jigsaw. If the audience had arrived on the Monday evening, those with seats in the front row would have had severely restricted views. The grass was thick and high and needed cutting and trimming. On the paved area, there was a small table, a chair and a sunlounger. A long branch hung over the set, made from steel tubes, soldered and bolted together, and wrapped in rope paper and painted. It was the longest apple tree branch on record. At the centre of the branch was an apple.

Simon Russell Beale entered in his whites and his pasties. The hair stylist, Adèle Brandman, had put heated curlers in his hair and rubbed in grease. Russell Beale stood in the green paved area and, as the cello played the high tinnitus sounds, he twiddled his new curls. He walked upto the beehive. Marcia Warren ran on in a black dress and brown shoes. The first laugh came after 10 lines when Felix distinguished between astronauts and cosmonauts.

Diana Rigg entered in her Jean Muir dress with her sunglasses, her G&T and no wig. When Rigg had entered during the technicals, wearing her Jackie Onassis wig, Caird saw at once that it was out-of-place. If only one person in a play is wearing a wig it suggests that the wig is a set-up and at some point in the story the wig is going to be removed. He thought the wig covered the laugh lines that run round Diana Rigg's cheekbones: one of her most expressive features. The wig was cut: her hair had simply been coiffed. Flora sat in the upright garden seat; there was no slouching in her Jean Muir. Mother and son approached their moment of closeness at the top of the play.

Backstage, one of the assistant stage managers, Andrew Speed, had accompanied William Gaunt underneath the rostra that support the grass mound. To reach his entrance behind the beehive, Gaunt had to crawl onto a level halfway up the rostra, get onto a ladder with padding on the top four steps, and climb through a small manhole. As Diana Rigg exited, the cello played the tinnitus sound again, and from the top of the grass mound came the clip-clip-clip of the secateurs. Gaunt appeared by the beehive and picked up blades of grass. He spoke to Felix about “Mrs Humble”, a detail that was added in rehearsals to help wrong foot the audience, and he pointed out a darkish-crimson rose, a Josephine Bruce. His shoes were white. At the technical rehearsal, Gaunt heard Russell Beale coming down the steps of the grass mound in his cornish pasties and knew at once that he'd have to change his brogues. The rostra amplified the sound like a drum. Gaunt wore the faded beach shoes that he wears when he gardens at home. In a south Yorkshire accent he spoke of the *bomblebees*.

The saxophonist switched from a soprano sax to an alto sax, which gave a jazzier, more American sound, and the music segued into Glenn Miller's ‘In The Mood’. Denis Quilley entered in a stripy shirt, carrying a jug of Pimms. The moustache that let the audience know that he was still *at it* had been waxed. He patted out the drum section on the cushion of the sun lounger, picked a rose – a large white one – and cried “bugger” as the thorn pricked him. Diana Rigg entered and Quilley had an abortive dance with her. This was a scaled-down version of a little routine that the other assistant stage manager, Valerie Fox, an ex-dancer, had devised in rehearsals. Quilley sipped his drink, listened to a willow warbler and whistled back. He put sun cream on Diana Rigg. Here were two actors playing a couple for the sixth time in their careers and it showed in the ease with which they played off one another. Rigg gave the rose back to Quilley as Russell Beale entered. Quilley stood with a white rose in his hand talking to the son of the woman he wants to marry. He explained that he was there to offer his condolences. The audience laughed. They didn't need to be Freudians to spot the phallic symbolism. Felix mocked George: “Used goods do have a special appeal”. The audience gasped at the speed of his cattiness. Here was a part that had been written for Russell Beale.

Diana Rigg brought on a present wrapped in birthday paper. On the auditorium's first level, John Caird jotted down his Theory of Jonesian Comedy: two plays run on parallel tracks, a funny one, and one that isn't at all funny. What's distinctive about *Humble Boy* is the speed with which it switches between the two. As soon as Russell Beale unwrapped the present some members of the audience were laughing. They knew the pot contained his father's ashes. The laughter was staggered as other members of the audience whispered to their neighbours *it's what?... it's the ashes!... oh!* Felix complained that his mother had wrapped his father up in happy birthday paper. Big laugh. Felix and Flora struggled over the pot, remembering the fight director's advice that Diana Rigg had to grab hold of Russell Beale's wrist rather than the pot itself. There was a tense moment at the end of the scene, when the stage was deserted. Charlotte Jones held her husband's hand as the cellist bounced her bow on one of the strings and a member of the stage crew flicked a switch. The apple did what it had failed to do a number of times during the technical rehearsals. It obeyed the law of gravity and fell the four metres from the overhanging branch into the long grass.

Cathryn Bradshaw entered with a crash helmet and picked up the apple. There would always be a spare one there if she couldn't find the one that had fallen. Russell Beale entered in his sunhat. This was the scene in which four hours pass in about 20 minutes. Some of the changes in the lighting were designed to be so slow and imperceptible, as dusk turned to night, that the cues themselves would last for seven minutes. The 300 lights had taken two days to plot. The lighting designer Paul Pyant had gone "big on gobos". They give the dappled effect of light through trees. Bradshaw asked Russell Beale to put the pot down and, when he did, she slapped him. It was the job of the person getting slapped to make the noise. Russell Beale had to think of it as two movements: (i) smack your hands (ii) bring your hands to your face. Rosie told Felix that she had a seven-year-old daughter. Laughter. Charlotte Jones smiled. The audience were following the plot. They were ahead of Felix. After Bradshaw and Russell Beale kissed, they headed into the long grass. Quilley entered and said that it was "a bloody desert out here" He undid his trousers and urinated on the paving. *Laughter. Disbelief. Distaste.* Was Denis Quilley actually peeing onstage? Quilley had a bag of water under one arm with a tube that went into his trousers. Inside his trousers he had a device for controlling the flow of water, and at the front of this device, the props department had provided him with a latex penis. Diana Rigg had walked into the rehearsal room one afternoon, as Quilley was attempting to master the controls and pee into a bucket, and said, "Just what one wants to see after lunch."

The first act was nearly over. Rosie told Felix that he was the father of her child and left. Felix was alone in the dark. The cello zithered, the piano shimmered and torchlight flickered through the grass. It was Jim looking for slugs. Felix opened his arms wide and said "b-b-b-bingo". Jim chuckled. The houselights came up. During the interval, the producer Matthew Byam Shaw, who had commissioned the play, wandered through the foyer listening to members of the audience... *if she's Ophelia, is he Polonius?... what else has she written?... was that his own pee?* The question uppermost in Byam Shaw's mind was *will this transfer?*

After the interval, Marcia Warren picked up the earthenware pot and put it on the lunch table. The audience were on to the joke at once. The size and speed of the laugh surprised Marcia Warren. She garnished the soup with the ashes. Big laugh. Denis Quilley poured out the wine and Cathryn Bradshaw raised her glass and lifted it so that Quilley gained an extra second as he moved round the table. The cast were halfway through prop hell. Russell Beale arrived in a grey suit that managed to be simultaneously baggy and tight-fitting. Big laugh. The sleeves had been lengthened that afternoon. He poured out some more wine, and the bottle was empty enough for him to be able to give Quilley the absolute dregs.

The soup was in the bowls and the actors had to wait twelve pages to eat it. In rehearsals there was a sense of *where is this going?* John Caird had said that he didn't believe the characters wouldn't get on and eat the soup. Charlotte Jones had said, "I think that Felix's line, that his mother hasn't been able to smell since his father died, is really important. It's the first mention of his father." In the first preview, Russell Beale delivered the line about his father as a *slamdunk*, as he called it, and everyone stiffened: Cathryn Bradshaw and Marcia Warren glanced at one another; Diana Rigg threw her full attention onto her wineglass; Denis Quilley clasped one hand to his forehead and studied his napkin. The characters preferred to switch the conversation to any topic – even the various ways of committing suicide – so long as no-one returned to the subject of the dead father. Text and subtext: what they were saying propelled what they weren't saying. At the first preview the types-of-suicide conversation picked up laugh after laugh. Diana Rigg lit up a Marlboro Light. The cigarette stayed in her mouth as she thanked Rosie for the "Nurse Pye nugget". Big laugh. Four of the cast ate the soup for 20 seconds or so before Diana Rigg asked Russell Beale to take the pot off the table. Marcia Warren's face was motionless – frozen in panic – and her hand hovered in the air. A big laugh, that went on and on. Warren grabbed the bowls and left, giving a little squeal on her final exit. There were 30 minutes to go.

Russell Beale moved his palm up and down as he tried to imagine a seven-year-old. Diana Rigg returned wearing a light blue cardigan. The evening had got cooler. Russell Beale produced the letter with the franking stamp from the Royal Entomological Society. James Humble had discovered a new species of bumblebee and named it after his wife. Diana Rigg reached the line that had made her want to play Flora. "When I was little I always thought I was marked out, special, that I was on the verge of something momentous. I used to tingle with anticipation." A bee chased Quilley off the stage as he exited to the latest music cue – a run of triplets on the piano – composed that afternoon.

William Gaunt appeared in a ghostly light and said, "Exit pursued by a bee." It was a literate audience and they laughed at the allusion to *The Winter's Tale*. But the atmosphere immediately changed. Flora could hear Jim. The temperature in the auditorium dropped as half the audience had an *omigod* moment: *Jim was James!* Gaunt led Diana Rigg towards the darkish-crimson rose, the Josephine Bruce. He walked up the steps into the darkness. Russell Beale returned. It was time to scatter the ashes. "I release my father to space..." He poured out the ashes – buckwheat flour and oats – to a silvery accompaniment from the piano. Diana Rigg picked up some plates and exited saying "Don't expect me to wave you off." Offstage she held on to the plates so that they wouldn't make the slightest sound. The saxophone and piano returned to the three-note theme. Russell Beale echoed the words of Hamlet, his last stage role, and said, "Let be". Russell Beale sat on the chair at the end of the table that Rigg had sat in, the one with the best sightlines. He repeated, "Let be." Fairylights appeared in the grass. In the control box, Fiona Bardsley said, "Lx cue 23 and sound cue 44... go." The first preview of *Humble Boy* was ending. There were four more performances before the First Night. The light on the beehive faded as the light on Russell Beale faded. There was the sound of a nightingale and the stage was black. The first performance was over.

The play opened six days later on 9 August 2001. Robert Butler's account of the first night and the play's reception can be found on www.nationaltheatre.org/publications from 24 August

Above: Mercy adds a little garnish to the gazpacho

Top: Mercy serves the gazpacho

Above: George finds his future happiness slipping out of his grasp

Right: Felix listens to his mother dismissing her husband's friends as "a group of tedious entomologists"

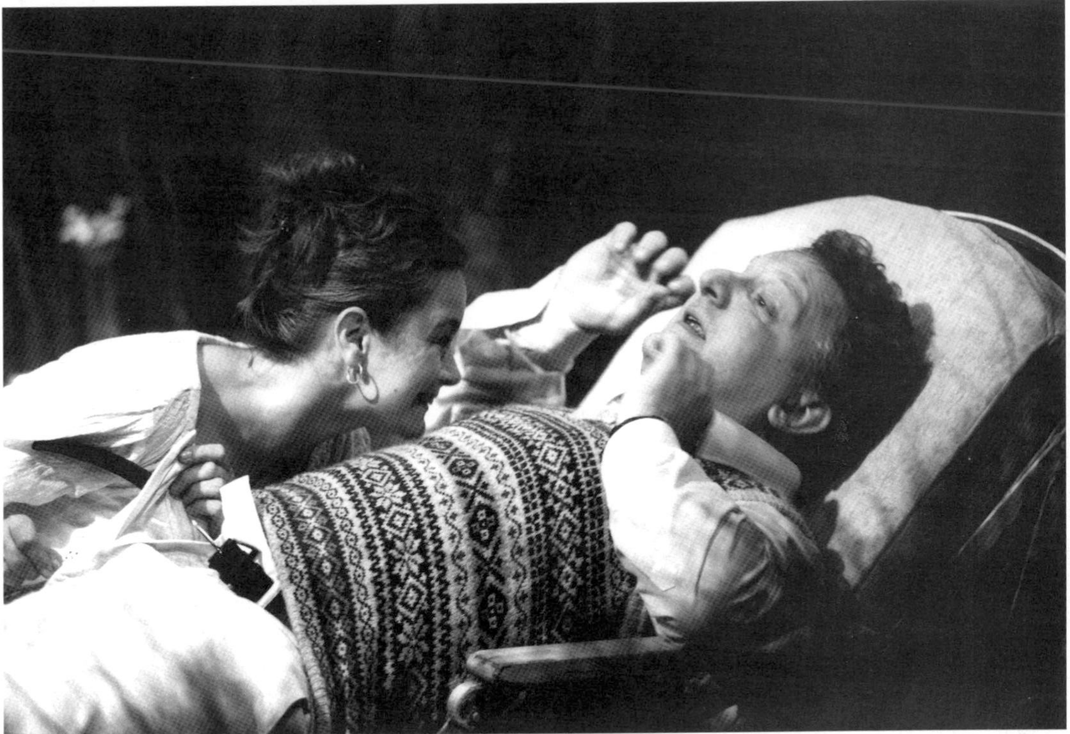

Left: Rosie returns to the Humbles' garden after seven years

Top: (George) So my advice to you, Humble Boy, is head for the skies.

Above: (Rosie) When was the last time you had sex?

Left: (Jim) You want to stop asking all the questions.

Above: Flora hears Jim's voice for the first time

Above: Jim leads Flora towards *Rosa Josephine Bruce*